THE ACID BATH MURDERER

A Terrifying True Story of one of the Worst British Serial Killer

by
Jack Rosewood

&

Rebecca Lo

ISBN-13: 978-1540308153

DISCLAIMER:

This true crime anthology includes quotes from those who were closely involved in the murder cases. It is not the intention of the author to defame or intentionally harm anyone involved. The interpretation of the events leading up to the capture and arrest of the murderers, or the suspicion of those uncaught, are the opinion of the author as a result of researching these true crime murder cases. Any comments made about the motive and behavior of the killers or the suspects is the sole opinion and responsibility of the person.

Free Bonus!

Contents

Introduction

John George Haigh will forever be remembered as the Acid Bath Killer. This cold and calculating serial killer didn't kill for love or revenge—he killed solely for money. Not in the sense of a contract killer though, but as a solitary killer who wanted to have the money he felt he was entitled to.

John was a child of a religious household, where the downsides of sinning were drummed into him every single day. He was restricted from associating with the general public and kept behind a high concrete wall erected by his father to protect the family from the outside world. You would think this would make John antisocial, but this certainly wasn't the case. In fact, he was so friendly and affable that he was able to wheedle his way into the lives of those above his social status and make them think he was one of their own.

Opposed to working legitimately for others and feeling he was entitled to a lot more money than he had, John set out on a career of rip-off schemes that would ultimately see him spend several stints behind bars. John liked the money he gained from these schemes, but he hated being caught and ending up in prison, so he needed a new plan—a plan that would see six innocent people lose their lives to fund John's lifestyle. A plan that would be so terrible that it would forever leave its mark in history.

It is one thing to take another person's life and bury them in a shallow grave somewhere, or to take them out to sea and throw them overboard. What John did with his victims was utter desecration of human remains. He believed that if there were no bodies he couldn't be charged with murder, and he came up with a disposal method that was both gruesome and shocking. John decided to use sulfuric acid.

CHAPTER 1:
An Unusual Childhood

In almost all serial murder cases, the first thing researchers and investigators analyze is the childhood and background of the killer. There has been much debate over the years as to whether or not someone is 'born to kill.' But, regardless of whether or not there are some who are born to be murderers, the role of the family, the lifestyle, and early childhood experiences are accepted to play a large part in the creation of a monster. This isn't to say that all who go through bad experiences as children become murderers—some overcome their terrible childhoods. But there are certainly those that don't, and John Haigh is one whose character and mindset was perhaps shaped by the environment he grew up in.

A Religious Home

John was born in England on July 24, 1909, to parents John Robert and Emily. Though born in Stamford, Lincolnshire, most of John's childhood was spent in Outwood, a village of West Riding, Yorkshire.

John's parents were members of a religious group called the Plymouth Brethren, also sometimes referred to as the Peculiar People. The Brethren were a Protestant sect who were very conservative. His father had built a wall around the property that rose 10 feet in height for the purpose of keeping out the 'outside world.'

John Senior was by any means a religious fanatic, and the young John was constantly reminded that he was being watched by a higher power. Because the sect was anticlerical and purist, all forms of social entertainment were banned. John was not even allowed to play sports, so his only entertainment at home was listening to endless bible stories and playing the piano.

Such was the devotion of John's parents to their religion, John's father believed the outside world was evil and the only way to protect the family was to keep them away from everyone else. This led to an extremely lonely childhood for John. His father had a blemish on his head that was blue in color, and his explanation was that it was the mark of a sinner, due to him misbehaving as a youth. This terrified John, as he did not want to be struck with the same mark. His mother on the other hand was deemed an angel because she carried no such mark.

The fear of being marked created a great deal of anxiety for young John. He would later claim to have been plagued by

4

gothic-like nightmares throughout his childhood, including dreams where trees would become blood-dripping crucifixes. However, John as an adult was known to be a liar and a good manipulator, so this may have been stated as a ploy to aid his insanity defense.

John's only company as a young child apart from his parents was his pets. He treated them very well and lovingly, and there were no signs at all that he showed any kind of cruelty or aggression towards them. He had great sensitivity to any person or animal he came into contact with. Many years later, after his arrest, he would claim to have shown that same love to his victims by killing them quickly without causing any suffering.

As a good child, there was rarely an occasion that required punishment. On those sparse occasions, John would be spanked by his mother using a hairbrush. John claimed that the bristles of the brush would draw blood, which he would then lick off the wound. Later he would claim that this was the trigger for his craving of the taste of blood.

One important turning point for John came about in his teenage years. By the time he was sixteen, he had indulged in activities his parents deemed to be sinful, yet they allowed him to do so. This proved to John that the fear of the blue blemish was nothing more than a story to instill fear in a young child. Knowing that he could get away with things without punishment was most likely what lead to his sociopathic behavior.

John developed the ability to be quick thinking and able to say whatever a person needed to hear to manipulate his way out of things. His remarks were clever, and he had learned to lie effectively with few people ever calling him out.

A Good Student

By all accounts, John was an intelligent student, regularly attending school and racing home afterwards each day to prevent being led astray by the 'evil' outside world. He won two academic scholarships—the first to Queen Elizabeth Grammar School, which was in Wakefield, and the second to Wakefield Cathedral, where he also became a choirboy. John had become quite an accomplished pianist and organist, and it seems that whatever he put his mind to, he could study and achieve without too much difficulty.

Not a lot is known about his time in school. It was perhaps the way of the times back then that as long as you turned up and did reasonably well that was all that mattered. It was a time when most young men left school at a relatively young age and entered the workforce or the armed forces. It is not surprising then that when John left school he didn't go on to further his studies. Instead he embarked on many different jobs and careers, some legitimate and others deceptively fraudulent.

Jack Of All Trades

When John left school, he became an apprentice at a motor engineering firm where he could indulge in his love of cars. However, John had an intense hatred of dirt, which made it difficult for him to cope in a garage setting, so he left after about a year.

John's next employment was with the Wakefield Education Community, where he worked as a clerk. This job didn't really suit John, and before long he had left that role and moved on to the next. At this time, he became an underwriter for insurance and advertising. In this role, he was rather successful for a short while, and what he learned about high finance enabled him to buy an Alfa Romeo—bright red of course—which at the time was a very expensive vehicle.

During his adulthood, John would go on to work in many different fields, which would enable him to pick up a variety of skills. Unfortunately, some of these skills when combined with his ability to be manipulative and deceptive would result in John crossing over into criminal activities.

CHAPTER 2:
John the Young Man

By 1934, things had really started to change for John. He no longer attended church, despite his parent's emphatic encouragement, and he had already been fired by one employer for theft. As a young man, John had begun to make decisions for himself that would set him on a deceptive and murderous journey through adulthood.

A Disastrous Marriage

John met a 21-year-old woman named Beatrice Hammer, commonly known as 'Betty', in 1934. It was a whirlwind romance, and they married after knowing each other for a very short time. Perhaps this was because John had the gift of gab and was always dressed well, giving an air of being more important or wealthier than he really was.

Betty was a very independent young woman, and some would consider her to be high-spirited. After she accepted John's proposal, they decided to keep the upcoming wedding news to themselves. She had begun to have second thoughts, unsure of John's true character having only known him for a short time, and she was also unaware of his financial situation. Despite these serious misgivings, she went ahead and married John on July 6, 1934.

Once wed, they moved into John's parents' house, which can't have been a pleasant experience for any of them really. It's one thing to live with the in-laws, but when they are religious fanatics like John's parents, it must have been a fairly oppressive atmosphere.

John decided he didn't want to work for another boss, so he started up his own business. Unfortunately, his business involved forging documents for vehicles, and before long, in October 1934, he was caught by the authorities. He was sentenced to fifteen months imprisonment, and by November of that same year, Betty had left him and filed for divorce.

While John was in prison, Betty had endured a pregnancy and labor on her own. When the baby was born, a little girl, she gave her up for adoption. John never got to see the baby and only ever saw Betty once more when he asked her to visit him in prison. He then stated that they had never been legally married, as he had another wife, but this was a lie. There has never been any mention or proof of a previous wife. Betty left and moved away so she would never have to see John again.

Walking a Criminal Path

Following his release from prison, John returned to his parents' home. He entered into the business of dry cleaning along with a partner, and for a while he seemed to stay on the right side of the law. The business was quite successful, and everything had turned around for John. Unfortunately, a tragic motorcycle accident resulted in the death of his business partner, and this led to the liquidation of the company. John was understandably disappointed and sour, and so he left home and headed to London.

Had the business survived, the future could have been very different—not just for John, but for the poor victims that crossed paths with him later on. He had tried to work legitimately, and it had failed. By now he had already done stints in prison, his wife had left him, his baby had been given away, and he had lost his business partner and his business. What more could possibly go wrong?

The Family Turns Their Backs

John's parents had never approved of his marriage to Betty, but they had done their best to help the young couple by offering them a home after their wedding. Neither John nor Betty was practicing religion, and this must have caused some tension.

However, it was John's imprisonment for fraud and the ramifications that it had on his marriage that really upset his parents. Not only was their son in prison, but his pregnant wife announced she wanted a divorce. To make things even worse, she then had the baby adopted out without consultation with anyone from the family. Prison, divorce, adoption—it's no wonder John's parents were becoming exasperated with him.

And they weren't the only ones. While he was still in prison, John was ostracized by the Brethren, unable to ignore his sins. Apparently John was completely shocked by this, and his mother was known to tell anyone who listened that this alone was going to affect John's future outlook.

After John lost the dry cleaning business and moved to London, his parents no longer had contact with him. Unwilling to be accepted by their religion and with all the legal and emotional turmoil they had already been through with John, they most likely reached their limit of tolerance.

CHAPTER 3:
A Deadly Acquaintance

In 1936, after arriving in London, things would start to spiral out of control in John's life. He would meet a man who would later become his first victim of murder. This man would also lead to two further victims, and John would embark on an even more flamboyant yet devious career move that would see him sentenced to more terms of imprisonment. It was during one of these stints in prison that John's horrible plan would be devised.

A Handyman for William McSwann

Once John had moved to London, he set about seeking some employment, and he came across an advertisement for a chauffeur at the local amusement park. He applied for the job, and on meeting the owner, William McSwann, he was hired on the spot. Most likely his application was successful because John did not disclose his criminal background.

John's role didn't just involve being a chauffeur. Because of his mechanical background, he also became responsible for repairs and maintenance of the amusement park machinery and equipment. John and William became good friends despite their roles of employer-employee. They had similar interests, including a love of fancy clothes and fast cars, and before long, William introduced John to his parents.

Donald and Amy McSwann liked John right away, and they were very pleased with how he undertook each task while working for their son William. In fact, John was such a good employee, he was promoted to the role of manager in a fairly short period of time.

After working for William for a year, John decided to move on to what he perceived to be bigger and brighter things. The McSwanns were all sorry to lose him as an employee, but John could never be happy working for someone else. Instead, he preferred to be his own boss.

John the Solicitor

When John left McSwanns' employment, he had come up with what he thought would be a surefire way of making money. He set up an office and presented himself to the public as a solicitor, and used the name of another company that had a good reputation to help secure clients. John had lied, saying he had an estate that he could liquidate and that he had public company shares he wished to offload.

On receiving checks from clients, John would proceed to cash them, but he never provided the goods they were supposed to be purchasing. Of course this was a difficult scheme to maintain over a long period of time, as ripped off clients would come knocking sooner or later. John tried to solve this problem by uprooting and setting up his scheme in other parts of London.

John's scheme worked for a while, but like all good things, it had to come to an end. Eventually, with all the reports from clients about being swindled, the police were able to track John down. Once again he was in front of a court on fraud charges, and this would send John back behind bars.

An Inmate Again

John was sentenced to four years for his stint as a fraudulent and thieving solicitor. Considering John wasn't highly educated, it's surprising that he was able to pull it off in the first place. This was perhaps a testament to just how intelligent he was. Or stupid, as he always seemed to get caught!

His time in prison seemed to go without a hitch, and when his sentence was up, he was released back into society. This freedom was not to last though, as within a year he was back in court. Once again John had stolen from someone and had tried to lie his way out of it when apprehended. However, he had quite a substantial record by now of fraud and theft charges, so his lies fell on deaf ears.

John was again sent to prison for a further twenty-one months. It was during this period of incarceration that John would dream up his most dastardly scheme yet—one that would put him in the history books and affect the lives of many people for years to come.

CHAPTER 4:
Crossing Paths Again

John was getting very tired of being locked up in prison all the time. After all, he had been caged behind bars on numerous occasions during his adult years, and he was frustrated that his dreams and plans of making money with minimal effort just weren't paying off. For John, it was time for a new plan—one that he thought would keep him out of prison for the rest of his life.

The Perfect Plan Concocted Behind Bars

While languishing in prison for twenty-one months, John had all the time in the world to formulate more schemes to make money. Because he had always had the misfortune of getting caught with every other scheme he had tried previously, his main focus this time was on gaining maximum profit with no chance of arrest.

John knew that it was easier to take money from others than make it himself, but this had often landed him in court. He therefore had to come with a way to carry out his plan without the risk. John decided he would target older, wealthy women.

After all, John was a dapper, charming man, and older women were typically lonely and easily led by a younger man.

John wasn't just planning on marrying or wooing these women and emptying out their bank accounts. This would leave behind a witness, and as he knew very well, this hadn't worked out well for him in the past. The only solution was to make sure there was nobody left behind to tell tales or give evidence. He would have to murder his targets.

For most people, the thought of planning and carrying out a murder would be unthinkable. But for John, it was a means to an end to ensure he got what he wanted and stayed out of prison. The only problem would be getting rid of the bodies. John believed that if there was no body, a person could not be charged with murder.

The prison had a metal shop, where inmates could learn skills or work during their imprisonment, and John learned that sulfuric acid was used regularly. He started working in the metal shop and learned how to handle and use sulfuric acid without causing himself any adverse effects or injuries. Finally, he felt he had come up with the perfect plan of how to get away with murder.

John needed to work out how much acid he would need to get rid of a body and how long it would take to do so. He enlisted the help of fellow inmates who provided him with mice, and used these to practice. John studied the effects of the acid on

17

the mice intently, calculating how much it took to get rid of each mouse and how long it would take for the job to be done efficiently. Interestingly, it took just half an hour to dispose of a mouse without any trace.

John believed he had finally come up with the perfect plan and waited patiently to be released back into the community.

William McSwann Disappears

In 1943 John was set free and launched back into society. He stayed on the straight and narrow for a while and was employed as an accountant for an engineering business. Weeks and months went by with John managing to stay out of trouble with the law, but his master plan was still very much on his mind.

As luck would have it, John ran into his old employer William McSwann in the summer of 1944. They enjoyed a drink or two in the local pub, and McSwann was very happy to see his old friend John. So happy in fact, that he insisted John accompany him to see his parents, who were also happy to see John.

The elder McSwanns enjoyed seeing John again, and during the encounter they made what would prove to be a fatal error in judgement. They told John all about the recent property investments they had made. But, to get to their fortune, John realized he would first have to take care of their beloved son— his friend, William.

John and William met up at a local pub in Kensington High Street called The Goat for a drink or two on 9 September. By this point in time, John had rented a workshop located at 79 Gloucester Road, and he was able to convince William to come and have a look.

Once inside the workshop, John picked up a blunt object and struck William over the head with it. To finish him off, he then slit his throat, and according John's diary filled a cup with his blood as it drained and drank it. William's body was placed into a 40-gallon drum and filled with concentrated sulfuric acid. The fumes were toxic and sickening, and John had to go outside for a while until they had settled. He then went back inside and placed a lid on top of the drum.

The following day, John went back to the workshop to check on the progress of the acid on the body. It had reduced the corpse to mere sludge, like lumpy liquid, and John proceeded to pour it all down a drain. The thought of having killed someone and successfully disposing of the body filled John with euphoria. He had carried out his plan, and it had worked.

The next part of the plan was all about profit, but it was going to take a little time. John visited William's parents straight after the murder and told them their son had run away and gone into hiding so he wouldn't be called up to serve his military duty. For almost a year, John regularly sent the McSwanns items and letters supposedly written by John, so they did not suspect a thing. It's remarkable that John was able to be patient for so long, but it wouldn't last forever.

Elder McSwanns Must Go

On July 2, 1945, John would execute the next step in his plan to gain access to the McSwanns' wealth. John had gone to visit the elderly couple at their home, and without warning murdered them in the same manner as their son. They were struck over the head to incapacitate them, and then their throats were slit. Once again John claimed to have drunk their blood.

They were transported back to his workshop where two drums of acid sat waiting. Both were placed into the drums and left to dissolve. Now he had to come up with yet another lie to explain their disappearance. He went to their landlady and informed her that the McSwanns had gone on a trip to America, and that all of their mail and William's needed to be forwarded on to him so he could take care of anything important for them.

John practiced signing William's name and set about gaining power of attorney over the McSwanns' properties and finances. Because of the ruse he had created about William hiding in Scotland, he was also able to collect William's pension checks. John had forged a property deed that had been owned by Mrs. McSwann, and by placing it under a false name he was able to sell it, making almost £2,000 in the process. This wasn't enough as far as John was concerned, so he set about selling all of the properties, possessions, and securities. Combined with the first property sale, John gained a fortune of around £6,000.

CHAPTER 5:
The Road Is Set

John had now committed multiple murders and had seemingly gotten away with it. He had money in his pocket, and was quite pleased to think his plan had worked so well. But, money doesn't last forever, especially if you are John Haigh, and before long he was scouting for his next victim. But first, it was time to move his operation to a new location.

John's Workshop

Like many other killers, John knew that it was a good idea not to stay in the same place for too long. For this reason, he rented a workshop located at 2 Leopold Road, Crawley, in Sussex. John equipped the small workshop with his possessions from the old workshop in Gloucester Road, including two 40-gallon drums and a large amount of sulfuric acid.

John was on the hunt for his next victim, as he was rapidly running out of money. He often stayed at a local hotel, the George Hotel, where he was constantly scoping out the residents and visitors for signs of wealth. Now that he had his disposal equipment set up at the workshop, there was nothing stopping him from carrying out his sinister plans, and he had an idea as to who his next victims would be.

The Henderson Murders

John had come to know Dr. Archibald Henderson and his wife Rose through a property deal back in 1947. The Henderson's had put their house on the market, and John had approached them, intending to learn more about their financial status. John was even prepared to offer the couple more than what their house was worth, and the Henderson's were so impressed with the charming John, they began to talk freely with him. Although their wealth was nowhere near the realm of the McSwanns', they nevertheless had enough money and property to whet John's appetite.

Meeting with them again in February 1948, John decided that the couple would be his next victims. Of course it can be difficult to kill two people at once, so he came up with a plan to separate them to make the job easier for himself. Like many before and after him, John decided that it was better to take out the male first, as they often put up the biggest fight.

He convinced Dr. Henderson that he had invented something the doctor should really see, and the two men drove from the Metropole Hotel in Brighton that the Henderson's called home to John's workshop in Crawley. Dr. Henderson obviously never suspected a thing, which is a testament to the charming personality John portrayed.

As soon as they arrived at the workshop and entered the building, John took out a revolver and shot Dr. Henderson in the head. Ironically, John had actually stolen the gun from Dr. Henderson's house earlier, which gives the crime an even more sinister tone. John then proceeded to place Dr. Henderson in the drum and fill it with the acid. Now to sort out his wife, Rose.

John went back to the Metropole Hotel and informed Rose that her husband had taken ill and that she must accompany him to her husband's side. The dutiful wife, Rose accepted John's offer of a ride, and they made their way to the workshop. Just like her husband, Rose was shot as soon as she entered the workshop and placed into a drum of acid.

Now John could carry out the rest of his plan. He returned to their hotel and paid their bill to make it look as though they had moved on. He also entered their room and took all of their valuables so they could be sold for profit. John wrote a letter pretending to be Dr. Henderson and was able to sell everything they had owned, gaining himself around £8,000. In today's finances, this would have been around £216,000! Strangely, John did keep the Henderson's dog, which could have been dangerous if anyone had noticed.

Rose's brother was sent letters forged by John to make him think the couple was still alive. He claimed in the letters that Dr. Henderson had performed an abortion, which was illegal, and to escape the law had fled to South Africa. John put quite a bit of effort into maintaining this falsehood, and when he gave some of Rose's clothes to his girlfriend, Barbara, he didn't tell her where they had come from. Most likely he told her he had bought them for her.

John had developed a sense that he was untouchable by the law, and he started to get sloppy with evidence. The acid hadn't worked quite as well on the bodies, and one of Rose's feet was still intact. Despite this, John tipped the drums out into the corner of the property's yard and seemed to make no effort to conceal any of it. John was becoming more confident and secure in his belief that he would never be caught.

Olive in the Drum

John had expensive tastes and a dangerous love of gambling, so by February 1949, his funds were once again running low. In that era, the money he had gained from the Henderson's should have kept him comfortable for a long time, but he insisted on living the high life.

John had been living at the Onslow Court Hotel in South Kensington for a few years, and had come to be acquainted with another long-term resident, who would not only bring him more money but would also lead to his downfall.

Mrs. Olive Durand-Deacon was 69 years old, a widow who had lived at Onslow Court for six years. Olive and John would exchange greetings and pleasantries when their paths crossed at mealtimes, and John had led her to believe he was an inventor and an engineer. He began to consider Olive as his next target, as she appeared to be very wealthy, often dressed in fur coats and dripping with jewels.

One day Olive mentioned to John that she had come up with an idea for creating false fingernails, and as an engineer and inventor could he help her make them so that they would be marketable. At first, John said that he would think about it. On the February 18, he invited Olive to his workshop under the pretense that he had been working on the false fingernail idea.

Like the others before her, Olive was shot in the head on entering the workshop. John took off her luxurious coat and valuable jewelry and put her into one of the drums. Once again, he filled the drum with acid and left Olive to dissolve. It would be two days before Olive was reported missing by a friend, Constance Lane.

CHAPTER 6:
Suspicions Abound

Olive Durand-Deacon was well known and well-liked by the other residents at Onslow Court, and it wouldn't be long before questions were being asked about her whereabouts. John approached her friend Constance and inquired as to whether she had heard anything about her missing friend. Remarkably, he even volunteered to drive Constance to the police station to report Olive missing. This one act put John in the line of sight of the investigating officers.

Criminal Record Points the Way

When his fellow residents had started asking questions about Olive's disappearance, John claimed that they had made an appointment to meet but Olive had not shown up. This more or less put him right into the middle of the investigation. If he had have just said he had no idea, rather than creating a story, he wouldn't have put himself into the situation he soon found himself in.

When John accompanied Constance Lane to the police station to report Olive as missing, a policewoman by the name of

Sergeant Lambourne was immediately suspicious of John. It is not clear why. Perhaps it was a gut instinct, but this led the investigators to take a look at John's background.

As part of the investigation, the local police contacted Scotland Yard on Monday, just a few days after Olive's disappearance, and made inquiries into the criminal past of John. At the same time, John had been a busy man. He had emptied out Olive's drum in the corner of the yard, just like he had done with the Hendersons' remains. He had also gone to nearby Horsham and had appraisals done on Olive's jewelry. On returning to Onslow Court, he was surprised to find the police waiting there for him.

When initially questioned, John again told his story that he had an appointment scheduled with Olive but she hadn't turned up. The police seemed to accept this story and left. However, they returned again on the Thursday and again questioned John. His story remained largely the same, but this time he added a few more details than he had previously.

The police decided to look at John's workshop, and on Saturday, February 26, they forced the door open and gained entry. They found empty and half-full carboys, which were ten-gallon glass bottles with narrow necks used to contain sulfuric acid, a rubber apron, and a gas mask. The police also found a .38 Enfield revolver that appeared to have been fired recently. In John's attaché case, they found a dry cleaning receipt for a black Persian coat made of lambskin—the very same coat they knew Olive had owned.

The report in the press encouraged the owner of a jewelry store in Horsham, Mr. Bull, to come forward to the police. He informed them that a man had brought some jewelry into his shop to be pawned on the day after Olive was reported missing. The police gathered the jewelry from the shop and took it to one of Olive's relatives, who immediately identified it as belonging to Olive. Although the ticket had been signed 'J. McLean', the jeweler's shop assistant recognized John as the man who had pawned the jewelry.

On the afternoon of Monday, February 28, John was met at Onslow Court by Detective Inspector Albert Webb. John was 'invited' back to the police station to help them with their investigation, and in a matter of hours John would start confessing.

A Horrifying Discovery

Dr. Keith Simpson, the Home Office pathologist, inspected John's workshop in Crawley on Tuesday, March 1. The first things he noticed were some bloodstains that were present on the walls. Inspecting the drums, he located a hat-pin at the bottom of one of them. He then investigated the yard.

In the corner of the yard was a pile of sludge, and Dr. Simpson noticed what appeared to be a human gallstone among the vile sludge. Suspecting the worst, he ordered the sludge to be collected and taken to the police laboratory for further analysis.

What that sludge contained would seal the John's fate. Although the acid had done a pretty good job of dissolving the bodies, unfortunately for John, it had not worked well enough to get him off the suspect list. In fact, the sludge contained multiple pieces of evidence, and despite there not being a complete body, there was enough to charge John with murder.

Analysis of the sludge uncovered the following evidence:

- 3 human gallstones
- 28 lbs. of human fat
- 18 pieces of human bone
- Portion of a left foot
- Dentures, both upper and lower
- A lipstick container
- Red plastic bag handle

Also found were two vertebral discs from a spine, a handbag, and a notebook, along with the hat-pin. Olive's dentist was called in to examine the dentures, and they were determined to be hers. The bone fragments from a foot were reconstructed and found to fit one of Olive's shoes. The evidence showed that without a doubt Olive had been murdered and dissolved in acid.

John's Confessions Don't Add Up

Now the police had evidence that John had killed Olive, and they also discovered paperwork in John's possession regarding the McSwanns and the Hendersons. When John was being questioned by Detective Inspector Webb, John straight out asked whether or not anyone would ever be released from the high security psychiatric hospital Broadmoor. Webb stated he couldn't discuss such a thing with John, and John then stated that if he told the detective the truth, he wouldn't believe him.

At that point, John confessed that he had killed Olive Durand-Deacon. He then went on to admit he had killed William McSwann, the elder McSwanns, and the Hendersons. But that wasn't all. John also confessed to killing three other people that the police knew nothing about. These three were a young man named Max, a woman from Hammersmith, and a young girl named Mary from Eastbourne.

The detective had warned John against speaking any further, but nothing was going to stop John from telling his story. After all, John believed that if there was no body, there could be no charge of murder, so he was happy to give all the details of what he did to each victim.

The first detailed confession was about Olive. John's statement regarding her murder took more than two hours to write, due to the amount of detail he gave. He explained that he had given her some paper to look at in the workshop that he claimed could be used to create the false fingernails. While she was looking at it, he took the revolver and shot her in the back of her head. John then went out to his car and got a glass and a penknife. He cut Olive with the knife and drained some of her blood into the glass and then drank it. Olive was then placed in the drum and the acid poured in.

He then went on to talk about the murders of William McSwann, the elder McSwanns and the Hendersons. John claimed that each murder was motivated by a lust for blood, though this was likely his way of building a case for insanity.

When talking about the elder McSwanns, he stated he had bashed them both with a piece of pipe and then drank their blood. John said the only reason he killed Mrs. McSwann was because her husband's body didn't provide enough blood to satisfy him.

Scattered amongst the murders of the McSwanns, the Hendersons, and Olive, there were the three mysterious murders John claimed to have committed. He did not provide the same level of detail or information on these three murders, and his claims were never substantiated. His confessions weren't adding up.

Why would he have so much detail about six murders but not three others? On the other hand, why confess to murders he may not have committed? Perhaps he thought the more murders he confessed to the better chance he had of dodging the gallows and instead spend his days in psychiatric care. Or, he was trying to prove he hadn't killed for financial gain.

CHAPTER 7:
The Judicial Process

John's trial was set to take place in July 1949. He was remanded into custody in the interim and told those that would listen that he did not kill for financial gain. It seemed extremely important for people to think his acts were random rather than planned, and this could be for only one purpose—an insanity defense.

The Trial Gets Underway

John was remanded into custody at the Horsham Police Station once he was charged with murder. His trial started on July 18, 1949, as it was the norm in those days for trials to take place almost right away, unlike today when it can take months. It was also to be an incredibly short trial, finishing the next afternoon!

The trial took place at what was originally called Lewes Assizes, later known as the Old Town Hall. Incredibly, up to 4,000 people tried to cram into the courtroom to watch the proceedings. Some even tried to illegally sell their seats, but that was quickly quashed by the police on guard.

Presiding over the trial was Mr. Justice Humphries, and the prosecution team included the Attorney General, Sir Hartley Shawcross, Gerald Howard and Eric Neve. Defending John were Maxwell Fyfe, David Neve (yes, Eric Neve's son!) and G.R.F. Morris. John was unable to pay for his legal team, so a deal was made with a journalist, Stafford Somerfield, whereby the 'News of the World' paper would pay for the lawyers provided John gave them an exclusive story.

The story and impending trial was so sensational that many newspapers were fighting to get the true story. One newspaper, however, pushed the limit too far and published sensitive information about John's crimes before the trial, which was illegal at that time. The Daily Mirror had focused on John's claims about drinking his victim's blood, so the defense counsel lodged a complaint against the paper.

The Daily Mirror editor at the time was Silbester Bolam, and he was threatened with contempt of court charges. The judge determined the publishers of the paper and the directors could also be charged. Bolam was found guilty and sentenced to three months in prison, and the company itself was fined £10,000 and court costs.

The first day of the trial was taken up by the prosecution putting forward their case, including the calling of 33 witnesses. The defense team failed to challenge any of the witnesses, and only four were questioned by cross-examination. By that afternoon, the prosecution was finished, claiming the murders had all been premeditated.

When the defense team presented their case, the one major witness called was questioned purely about John's mental state. It was clear the defense was going to try and prove John was insane.

During the trial John had focused most of his attention on a crossword puzzle and not once attempted to speak for himself. The only time he paid attention was during the summation at the end of the trial, with the defense determined to prove he was insane and the prosecution working just as hard to prove that he was not.

The summing up by the judge took an hour, during which he instructed the jury to ignore John's admission of guilt regarding the murder of Olive Durand-Deacon. Instead, they were to focus on whether or not the prosecution team had proven his guilt.

The Insanity Defense

John had pleaded insanity, as was expected. He relied on his claims of drinking the victim's blood to try and reinforce that he was insane. He claimed he had disturbing dreams as a child, filled with images of blood. These dreams involved blood oozing from trees in a forest, and this blood was collected in a cup by a man who urged John to drink.

One of the defense witnesses was Dr. Henry Yellowlees, a physician who stated he found John to have a paranoid constitution. He found John's demeanor when talking about his crimes was one of indifference and something he had never seen in a person before.

Despite Dr. Yellowlees being convinced that John was suffering from a type of mental illness, he was unable to say without a doubt that John did or did not know the right from wrong. Therefore, he could only talk about his opinion of John's mental state from interviewing him.

When put under pressure on the stand, Dr. Yellowlees had to admit that he hadn't spent a great deal of time interviewing John. In fact, the total amount of time they had spent together only amounted to two hours. This meant that he could only really base his diagnosis on how John presented himself at the time. At the crux of this problem was an admission by John that he had a habit of drinking his own urine—a habit that many would assume could only belong to a madman. But, throughout his time in prison, he was only ever seen to drink it once, so this was most likely a sham to try and convince the doctor and the court that he was insane.

Despite the defense team's best efforts, the Attorney General told the jury they needed to reject an insanity plea, as John's actions showed malice before each murder. This meant that the crimes were premeditated and not the random act of someone who was insane.

Conviction and Sentence

The entire trial took a little over twenty-four hours, and the jury deliberated for just seventeen minutes before coming to a conclusion. The overwhelming forensic evidence and the failure of the defense to prove insanity resulted in John being found guilty of the murders. John was sentenced to death and sent to Wandsworth Prison to await his execution.

Because of the severity of the sentence and the seemingly unanswered questions regarding John's mental health, a medical inquiry was ordered by the Home Secretary under the Criminal Lunatics Act of 1884. To undertake this inquiry, three renowned psychiatrists were assigned to the task.

Each of the psychiatrists thoroughly examined John's case and all agreed that there was no sign of insanity and that John had simply been 'acting'. They could find no proof of mental illness or defect, and therefore concluded that John was and had been sane when committing the murders. Satisfied with the outcome, John's sentence was left in place.

As agreed with the newspaper that paid his legal bill, John did finish the story of his life during his incarceration. He wrote letters to his parents and his girlfriend, Barbara Stephens.

John and Barbara had planned to marry before his arrest, and she was deeply affected by John's trial and sentencing.

To try and understand what had gone wrong with John, Barbara visited him often while he was in prison. She even asked him if he had planned on killing her as well, which must have been weighing on her mind. Had he seen her as another of his targets? John insisted that it had never crossed his mind, that what was between them was genuine.

John's parents were rather old by the time he was incarcerated, and they were never able to come and see him before his execution. His mother had sent greetings to John via a reporter, instead of replying by letter. John told Barbara that he believed in reincarnation and that his mission wasn't finished yet, so he would be coming back. This was perhaps the most chilling thing he ever said.

A famous waxworks in England, Madame Tussaud's, asked John if he would agree to being fitted with a death mask so they could recreate a waxwork figure of him. John easily agreed, probably because it would increase his notoriety and stroke his ego, even though the figure wouldn't be completed until after his death.

John made a rather strange request to one of his jailers before his execution. He asked if they could do a trial run of his execution so they could make sure everything would go smoothly without hitch. This either didn't go any further or was denied, as it never took place.

On August 10, 1949, John was taken to the gallows and hanged by the Chief Executioner, Albert Pierrepoint. All of his clothing was bequeathed to Madame Tussaud's so it could be adorned by his waxwork figure in the Chamber of Horrors. Typical of John, he left instructions that the clothes must remain in perfect condition, including creases in the trousers. He also insisted his 'hair' be parted a particular way and that the cuffs of his shirt should be showing. Even in death, he tried to stay in control and ensure his 'dapper, charming' outward appearance be maintained, even if it was only on a wax creation of himself.

CHAPTER 8:
Killing For Greed

There are many different motives for murder, the most common being emotions such as love, jealousy or anger. Sometimes, there is more than one motive—such as killing a spouse for financial gain—where the emotion of anger or hatred is combined with greed. But in some cases, the pure motive is that of gaining money, such as was the case with John.

Not the Only One

John was certainly not the only murderer in history who killed to get money. Undoubtedly, there will be many more to come, too. But there are different forms of killing for financial gain, and although all murders are atrocious, there are certain types of greed killings that are more disturbing than others.

When a wife or husband goes missing, the first thing investigators often look into is whether or not the other spouse is involved and if there is an insurance policy on the missing person's head. Killing a spouse to get their insurance money is probably the most common form of killing for greed. Plus, if you no longer want your spouse around, it's a convenient way of killing two birds with one stone, so to speak.

Likewise, there have been cases of business partners taking out their associates so they can gain full financial control and benefits of a company. Often though, they also despise the person they kill, so this combines an emotional motive with greed. When this occurs, it is important to try and identify what the principal motive was—hatred for the person, or the money they will gain if that person is no longer around. Often, it is the money that creates the stronger motivation.

Armed robbery that ends in murder is another form of killing for financial gain, but they generally don't plan to kill, and the murder occurs because of circumstance, be it panic or perceived threat from the person they are robbing. This is a truly senseless form of murder for money, as there is no emotional connection between the killer and the victim. It's simply a case of greed and the need for self-preservation.

In almost all of these situations there is just one victim. Serial killers who murder purely for greed are not as common, but John most certainly fits this category. There was no emotional factor in the murders and there had been no wrongs committed against John by the victims—he just wanted their money.

Estimated Financial Gain

Apart from the money John gained from his illegal activities, including multiple cases of fraud, he gained a large amount of money from his murder victims. The murder of William McSwann was the training run for John to see how long and how effectively the acid would dissolve his body. The real target was William's parents, because if he got rid of them he could gain their wealth as well as William's. While they still believed William was alive and just in hiding in Scotland (as John had convinced them), John was unable to gain control of William's finances.

Once the elder McSwanns had been murdered as well, John was able to start collecting William's pension checks, which provided a regular source of income. He also gained control through deceit over the financial affairs of the McSwann family and began selling off everything they had owned. Overall, it is estimated John gained about £8,000 from the McSwann estate.

Dr. Henderson and his wife Rose had been very forthcoming with John about their wealth and financial affairs, including property they owned. This ultimately sealed their fate, and John didn't hesitate to kill them both to fund his lifestyle. Well-practiced in the art of forgery, John was able to sell off the belongings and property of the Hendersons and keep the funds.

His financial gain from their murders totaled £8,000. And he kept their dog.

Finally, John thought that killing Olive Durand-Deacon would net him potentially his biggest financial gain. After all, Olive was very refined, wore fur and lambskin coats, and was always adorned by glittering jewels. She more or less oozed a sense of privilege and money. Unfortunately for John, he was unable to carry out the rest of his plan due to his arrest. Therefore, he only gained about £110 from the death of Olive and an end to his own mortality.

Premeditated Evil

There are few known serial killers that put as much thought and planning into their crimes as John did. The fate of his victims was determined long before any of them had even met John. They were simply pawns in his long-term plan to gain enough money to not have to work legitimately.

From young adulthood John had constantly come up with numerous money-making schemes in the hopes of making as much money as he could without minimal effort. The first few schemes he put into action weren't successful for a long period, as he always seemed to get caught in his illegal ploys.

Many conmen spend years honing their craft so they can get away with their schemes for as long as possible, but John was quick to move on to the next plan after each failure, rather than putting more thought into it. After multiple brushes with the law and periods of incarceration, John knew it was time to come up with a better way to fleece money from people.

As far as is known, John first came up with the plan to commit murder during his last incarceration for fraud. What made him cross the line from committing fraud to contemplating murder is unknown. Most conmen stay within the confines of fraud and theft, rather than killing for money. But for John, it seemed to him to be the perfect plan.

For the first time in his life, John was meticulous in his planning processes, contemplating not only the actual killing of the victim, but also how to dispose of the body and use their paperwork to steal their money and property. The fact that he even went so far as to practice disposing of mice using acid while in prison shows how much premeditation was involved in what would become a spate of terrible murders.

Each of John's known victims was the result of evil premeditation. He planned who he was going to kill, where, when, how, and what he would have to do to get rid of any evidence. He also planned in advance how he would gain access to their finances, in some cases concocting wild stories to cover up disappearances, and fraudulently assuming the victim's identity to forge papers.

John was a cold, calculating murderer with a complete lack of empathy for his victims and their families. Not once did he hesitate to put a bullet in his victims, including his good friend William McSwann—a man he had spent a lot of time with over the years and who had introduced John to his own family. Unfortunately, this friendship sealed not only his own fate, but also that of his elderly parents, as John added them to his murder list.

Some people could argue that a killer such as John is even more disturbing than a serial killer who murders random people, simply because of the interaction between John and his victims. John befriended each and every one of them over a period of time, placing himself comfortably within their lives, all the while knowing that he was going to eventually kill them.

CHAPTER 9:
The Big Questions Remain

In some ways the speed at which trials were conducted and execution sentences carried out in those days was a good thing, but on the other hand, it often left many questions unanswered. Over the last few decades, more effort has been put in to interviewing killers from a forensic psychology point of view, which has led to more understanding of why they kill and finding answers to questions that may remain after trial. In John's case, his sentence was carried out very quickly, so there were a lot of puzzling questions that were left unanswered.

Were There Others?

During John's initial police interview, he confessed to a total of nine murders. This baffled police, as they only knew about the six that had been disposed of in the drums of acid. But John claimed he had also killed a young man named Max, a woman named Mary from Eastbourne, and another lady from Hammersmith.

Despite their best efforts, the police were unable to substantiate any of these claims. In fact, there was nothing to suggest these three people had even existed. The only close possibility of another victim was related to the alleged theft and destruction of John's vehicle in June 1948.

John owned a Lagonda, and after he reported it missing it was located at the bottom of a cliff, apparently having been either pushed or driven off the edge. Within a month, the body of a female was found near the wrecked car, and she has never been identified. Despite his ease at confessing to the other murders, John always claimed he knew nothing about his car nor the body found nearby.

John had been overheard stating he wished someone would steal the car, so people naturally thought that he had destroyed the car himself by pushing it over the cliff. After all, it was insured, and he was quick to replace it with a new one. He had even taken Barbara Stephens to look at the wreck and told her not to tell anyone about it, which raised her suspicions. So the question was, did he simply pull an insurance job on his car, or was the female body a victim he was trying to dispose of? Perhaps he thought the car would catch on fire and destroy the physical evidence. Nobody really knows for sure.

General consensus in the legal community was that the extra three murders John confessed to were fictitious. They simply did not fit the pattern of his other murders. There seemed to have been no planning involved in their deaths, and John didn't seem to even know who they were. With his other victims, he made it his mission to find out all he could about them before he killed them.

These mysterious three victims were random killings according to John, which goes against every other murder he committed. It is unusual for a killer to commit both random and planned killings, except for cases where a serial killer may turn on a family member or remove a witness.

There was also no apparent financial gain from killing these three people. As we have already determined, John's whole purpose for killing was for financial gain, so why would he have bothered taking the lives of these three alleged victims? If these murders didn't take place, there could be another very good reason why John would invent them.

John's entire defense strategy was to try and convince the judge and jury that he was insane. Because he had killed six people for financial gain this wasn't proof of insanity, as there was a reason for him to kill each person. But, if he could persuade the police and legal system that he had killed three additional people without any financial gain, then there could be an argument made that he had committed all murders because he was insane.

Unfortunately for John, this part of his plan hadn't been thought through quite enough to be successful. For a man with a mind that recalled small details, he couldn't relay enough information regarding these three mystery murders to make them plausible. He couldn't recall anything about these victims except for a couple of names, Mary and Max, which themselves were common.

Because of this, there was no way to confirm whether these murders had ever occurred or not. There were no missing persons reports in those areas that fit the descriptions given by John, and there were no bodies found where he stated the murders had taken place. By his own admission, John had made no attempts to conceal or dispose of these bodies, so if he had indeed committed these murders, the victims should have been found.

But John didn't stop there in his efforts to show he was insane. His next explanation for committing the murders was even more bizarre than confessing to three supposed imaginary murders.

Vampiric Tendencies or Fantasy?

What better way to convince people that you're insane than by regaling tales of blood lust triggered by Gothic nightmares? Or at least that's what John thought. His final ploy to show he was insane lead to fantastic headlines of 'vampirism', and this became the main focus of the general public. Fear reigned, as the community contemplated the thought of a modern-day vampire roaming the very cobblestoned streets they themselves strolled each day.

During his psychiatric evaluations John claimed to have been plagued with terrible nightmares since childhood that would become a trigger for his need to consume blood. According to John, these dreams would consist of trees transforming into crucifixes weeping with blood and a man collecting the blood in a cup and trying to make John drink it. Of course there is no way to determine whether or not these dreams were real or if they were a figment of John's imagination. Even if they had troubled his sleep for years, there is no correlation of such a nightmare forcing or creating a need for blood in real life.

To confuse things even more, John also claimed that his taste for blood came from punishments inflicted by his mother when he was a young child. She would allegedly smack him on the hand with a hairbrush when he was naughty, and he would lick the blood drawn by the bristles of the brush. This according to John made him associate the harsh religion of his parents with physical violence and the taste of blood.

John had gone so far as to keep a diary, supposedly updated after each murder he committed. According to the diary, while he was with William McSwann he developed a sudden need to drink blood, and this was why he struck William in the head. He then slit his throat and collected the blood in a cup before drinking it. When questioned by the police and the psychiatrists later, he claimed to have drunk some of the blood of each of his victims.

By giving two completely different causes for his apparent blood lust, the dreams and the punishment by his mother as a child, John had accomplished nothing more than convincing the authorities that he was making it all up. His plan had completely backfired. If he would have stuck to just the one, such as the terrible nightmares, his story would have seemed more plausible.

Numerous psychologists and doctors examined John on the basis of determining sanity, and a man claiming to be a vampire of sorts was even more intriguing to them, as it certainly wasn't something you heard every day. However, the concurrence between physicians was that a compulsion to drink blood is associated with sexual deviation, and John exhibited no signs of being a deviant. In complete opposition, John apparently had very little interest in sex at all, so he definitely did not suffer from such a disorder.

Also, during John's time in the police cells and later in prison, not once did he ever show an interest in the need to drink blood. If he really wanted to try and convince everyone he had some sort of vampiric disorder, he probably should have continued the ruse while in custody.

Complete Disregard

John would easily fit the description of having a psychopathy, more commonly referred to these days as antisocial behavior disorder. He showed no remorse or guilt for the crimes he committed and no empathy for the families and friends of his victims and the pain he inflicted upon them. His moral compass was completely flawed, and he paid no consideration to the feelings of others.

It was as though John felt that he was above the law, and he had no respect for the laws or the legal system. He felt that he was too clever to be caught, and his sense of self-importance was heightened in comparison to the reality. The way John dressed, the cars he owned, and the way he portrayed himself to others was way above his actual social standing. Many who met John thought he was upper class, a charismatic gentleman, and therefore no threat.

John's only concern in life was himself. He had an exaggerated sense of worth and felt that he was entitled to the riches that others had. He saw absolutely nothing wrong with taking what he felt he should have, and he gave no thought to the people who would be affected by his actions. It didn't matter to John who you were, provided you had money. If you had it, he wanted it.

Some may think that he killed for money because he was lazy and didn't want to earn an honest living. However, he had held down legitimate jobs on occasion without too much difficulty. He was most definitely greedy, always wanting more and more money, but what was at the root of this greed? Was it laziness, an elevated sense of entitlement, or was it borne from his strictly religious upbringing?

In reality, the monster that was John could have been created by a combination of these. John wasn't a problem at school, and the jobs he held, including his employment with William McSwann, he undertook well, with no complaints from his employers. Although there was some theft from one employer, his work ethic was not in question. So considering the possibility of laziness, this seems less likely. He could certainly work if he wanted to.

John's feelings of being better than he really was could have come from a variety of sources, but most likely started at home. As an only child, he would have had the sole focus of his parents. Often in homes where there is only one child, the parents over-compensate and spoil the child, whether by material things or attention.

The fact that John was very isolated from the outside world as a young child by his parents religious beliefs could have caused him to have little empathy for others. As a child he seemed to care more for his pets than for people, probably because they were always there and looked up to him as a master.

It can be too easy sometimes to blame things on a religious upbringing, but in John's case, it was at the extreme end of religion. His parents were zealots and did everything they could to teach John the right ways to journey through life.

There were many restrictions placed on John, and he was sheltered from the real world and all its apparent sinning by a huge wall his father built around the home.

Those who practice religion to the same extreme as John's parents often live very frugally, just getting by on what they need rather than what they want. There wouldn't have been fancy clothes, apart from church clothes, or parties or luxuries at all. This could have been a contributing factor to John's need to have more—a sports car, flashy clothes, and any other items that indicated he had lots of money.

It is easy to speculate on what was the driving force behind John's crimes, but unfortunately hindsight doesn't always answer every question. What was truly going on in John's head will never be known, as he was executed before any further examinations could be made. In today's society, where a convicted killer could spend their life behind bars—or at least a decade waiting for an execution date—there is more time to investigate the mind of a killer. But, in 1940s England, there just wasn't enough information and knowledge to come to a firm conclusion regarding his actions and his motives.

CHAPTER 10:
Wandsworth Prison

Between the years of 1878 and 1961, Wandsworth Prison was the site of 135 executions. Of these, only one was a woman and nearly all were for the crime of murder. There is a lot of history associated with Wandsworth, and it is still being used today, although executions are no longer carried out. John spent his final days incarcerated at Wandsworth, and understanding the place and the execution process he experienced helps to further tell his story.

The History of the Prison

Originally, Wandsworth prison was called the Surrey House of Correction when it was built in 1851. It was a major construction, spanning 26 acres, but by 1870 they were running out of space, so they made the incredible decision to remove the toilets from the cells. From that time right up until 1996, prisoners were forced to use 'buckets', and the practice of emptying them became known as 'slopping out'. The stench within the prison must have been appalling and horribly unhygienic.

Up until 1878, all executions were carried out at the nearby Horsemonger Lane Gaol, but when it closed these duties were shifted to Wandsworth. At that time there was just one single condemned cell, so when more than one man was sentenced to death at a time, they would often be held within the hospital wing of the prison.

The Gallows and the Hangman

When Wandsworth prison took over executions, they had to build an execution chamber which would become known as 'The Cold Meat Shed'. Within this shed was the gallows, which had been brought to the prison from Horsemonger Lane Gaol. This original chamber and gallows consisted of beams that were positioned 11 feet above the trapdoors. Beneath the trapdoors was a pit, 12 feet deep and lined with bricks.

In 1911, the prison stopped using the original execution chamber and built a new two-story facility beside the condemned cell. The first floor of the facility contained the beams and trapdoors, and the second floor was primarily for the removal of the body following the execution.

The third and final execution chamber was built in 1937, using three existing cells situated one above the other. The top floor housed the beam and the trapdoors, which were 9 feet long by 5 feet wide. There were also ropes for the wardens to hang onto while supporting the prisoner. The bottom floor was obviously for the removal of the body and was known as the 'drop room' or 'pit room'.

Witnesses often commented on how clean the execution suite was, with its varnished floors and tidiness. Despite executions stopping in 1961, the gallows were regularly checked every six months right up until May 1993, when they were dismantled. This testing continued in case the death penalty was ever resurrected for cases of treason, mutiny in the Armed Forces, or piracy with violence. Nowadays the execution chamber has been converted into a rest room for the staff of the prison.

The first four executions at Wandsworth prison were carried out by William Marwood, from 1878 to 1882. The next executioner was Bartholomew Binns, though he only carried out one execution. James Berry executed the next six prisoners from 1885 to 1891. From there the job became a family affair, with James Billington hanging nine prisoners and then handing the reigns over to his sons, John and William. The two younger Billington men executed four men each before the next family took over.

Henry Pierrepoint became executioner after the Billington brothers, and he executed a total of six. Henry's brother Tom then hanged 27 men before handing the role on to his son Albert. Up until 1955, Albert Pierrepoint executed 48 prisoners, including John Haigh. Following on from the Pierrepoints, the next executioner was a man named John Ellis, who executed eight prisoners, and Robert Baxter went on to execute another nine. The last four executions to take place at Wandsworth were conducted by Harry Allen.

Infamous Inmates

Having been in existence for such a long time, Wandsworth has been home to numerous infamous inmates, from spies to robbers to murderers. John Haigh was one of many to have lost their lives to the gallows at Wandsworth, but even more have been incarcerated for a variety of crimes and escaped the hangman's noose.

Notable Inmates:

Charles Bronson (Charles Salvador) – armed robbery and violence

Bruce Reynolds – organizer of the Great Train Robbery

Christopher Tappin – selling weapons to Iran

James Earl Ray – assassination of Rev. Dr. Martin Luther King Jr. (remanded)

Julian Assange – remand

Max Clifford – indecent assault, eight counts

Oscar Wilde – gross indecency with men (sodomy)

Ronnie Biggs – the Great Train Robbery

Ronnie Kray – organized crime

Gary Glitter – sex offender

As well as these inmates, Wandsworth has also housed many murderers, which include:

George Chapman (born Severin Klosowski)

Chapman was convicted of murdering three of his girlfriends by poison between 1897 and 1902. An autopsy of the final victim, Maude Eliza Marsh, showed evidence of a lethal dose of a poison called tartar emetic. He was executed within three weeks of his trial, on April 7, 1903, by William Billington.

Albert Ernest and Alfred Stratton

These two young men were convicted of killing an elderly couple, Thomas and Ann Farrow, during the commission of a robbery on March 27, 1905. The victims had been bashed to death, and for the first time ever a fingerprint was used to prove guilt. Albert, who was only 20, had left a fingerprint on the cash box, and although the jury was instructed not to convict on that evidence alone, both men were found guilty. They were executed at the same time on May 23, by John Billington who was assisted by John Ellis and Henry Pierrepoint. The height and drop calculations were not accurate, and as a result, Alfred's neck was not broken cleanly, resulting in him dying from asphyxia instead.

William Henry Kennedy

Along with Frederick Guy Browne, William Kennedy was arrested and convicted of the murder of police constable George

Gutteridge. Even though Kennedy hadn't actually killed the officer, he was convicted of the crime because he admitted he had been there that night, known as 'doctrine of purpose'. Although they were sent to different prisons, both men were hanged at the same moment on May 31, 1928. Kennedy was hanged at Wandsworth by Thomas Pierrepoint, with the assistance of Robert Wilson.

Gordon Frederick Cummings

During the space of one week in February 1942, Airman Cummings murdered four women and was in the process of killing a fifth when he was discovered. He made a run for it but left behind his gas mark, which had his name and rank labelled on it. Fingerprints were matched at each of the murder scenes, and he was convicted on April 27. On June 25, he was hanged by Albert Pierrepoint and his assistant Harry Kirk.

Derek Bentley

The case against Derek Bentley was deeply controversial and became a focal point of the anti-capital punishment movement. He had participated in an armed robbery at a factory, during which a police constable, Sidney Miles, was shot and killed. Bentley was hanged on January 28, 1953, by Albert Pierrepoint. He was eventually granted a pardon posthumously in 1998.

Francis Forsyth (Flossy)

On June 25, 1960, Forsyth was one of four young people who killed a man named Allan Jee by beating and kicking him to death. The group was seen fleeing the crime scene, and Forsyth made the mistake of boasting about the murder, leading to an associate giving the names of all four youths involved to the police. Forsyth and another youth, Norman James Harris, were both convicted of capital murder. Similarly to the case of Browne and Kennedy, Forsyth and Harris were executed at the same moment but at different prisons. Forsyth was executed at Wandsworth on January 28, 1953 by Albert Pierrepoint.

Guenther Fritz Podola

Podola had committed a robbery of a woman by the name of Mrs. Schiffman in July 1959, and he attempted to blackmail her by saying he had tape recordings and embarrassing photos of her. She didn't believe him and reported it to the police, who put a trace on her telephone for the next time he called. They were able to trace it to a phone box, and he was quickly caught. However, as one policeman went to retrieve the car, Podola pulled out a gun and shot Detective Sergeant Raymond Purdy, and ran away. Ironically, when Purdy's belongings were returned to his widow, they included Podola's address book that Purdy had confiscated, which led police straight to him. He was tried and convicted, and on November 5 1959, he was hanged by Harry Allen.

Hendrick Neimasz

Neimasz was to be the last murdered hanged at Wandsworth prison. He had been convicted of the murders of Mr. and Mrs. Hubert Buxton, which took place on May 12 1961. He was hanged by Harry Allen with the assistance of Samuel Plant on September 8 1961.

CHAPTER 11:
The Truth About Sulfuric Acid

For the average person, the thought of plunging a human body into a barrel of acid is abominable. Having to deal with the fumes, smells and horrifying sludge that's left behind would be enough to put the majority of people off even disposing of a dead animal in this way! But where did the idea of using acid to dispose of bodies even come from?

The Effects on the Human Body

The acid used by John to dissolve his murder victims was sulfuric acid, often spelt 'sulfuric'. This is the strongest of the acids, being highly corrosive, and used to known as 'oil of vitriol'. To look at it is usually a slight yellow color or clear, but sometimes a dark brown dye is added so that it is recognized easily as a hazard.

Sulfuric acid is soluble in water, regardless of the strength of its concentration, and the higher the concentration, the more destructive it is. One of the most common uses of sulfuric acid is in drain cleaning agents, but it is also used extensively in a variety of industries including fertilizer production, oil refining, mineral processing and wastewater processing.

This acid decomposes lipids and proteins when it comes in contact with flesh and skin due to ester and amide hydrolysis. The water from the acid solution causes a reaction with the fats and proteins of the body, and these are broken down into a sludge or slurry of fatty and amino acids. The acid also causes a catalyst with the hydroxyapatite found in bones, reducing them to a solution of phosphate and calcium.

Although sulfuric acid can be successful in breaking down human tissue, it never completely destroys the entire body. There will always be parts left behind, even if only on a microscopic level. Bone fragments, gallstones, dentures and other hard parts of the body can often be found amongst the sludge.

When using sulfuric acid, there is a great risk of not only spilling it on your skin or getting it in your eyes, but also severe lung damage from inhaling the fumes. When John used it, he used to run from the room as quickly as possible, and wouldn't enter the workshop again until the fumes had dissipated. Even just inhaling the fumes can be lethal.

How Did John Attain So Much Of It?

In John's day it was much easier to obtain large quantities of chemicals including sulfuric acid. Because he had a workshop, he could have claimed it was for metal working or cleaning uses, and these things were not followed up as they would be today. At one point John had obtained 3 carboys of acid (also called a demijohn or a jimmy john), which is a rigid container that holds up to 60 liters (16 US gallons) of liquid.

Nowadays it is very difficult to purchase sulfuric acid, particularly in large amounts. The sale and purchase of this acid is controlled by the United Nations, under the United Nations Convention Against Illicit Traffic in Narcotic Drugs and Psychotropic Substances act of 1988. This is because sulfuric acid is a major ingredient for the manufacture of narcotics and psychotropic substances.

Although it is possible to buy sulfuric acid with certain restrictions, what is normally available is a weakened version. It is almost impossible to buy pure sulfuric acid, even for those industries that need it. It became even harder in the last 10 years as the world became more aware and alert to the threat of terrorism, as sulfuric acid can be used in the manufacture of bombs.

So, although it appeared to be easy for John to purchase large quantities of the acid, if he had been alive today, things may have been a lot more difficult for him to carry out his criminal acts. Not impossible mind you, as acid has played a part in some murder cases in recent times.

Modern Day Murder Cases

Although John Haigh is the most famous murderer who used acid to dispose of his victims, he certainly hasn't been the only one. In recent years there has been quite a spate of murders involving the use of different types of acid as a method of body disposal. One of the most gruesome cases took place in Australia in 1999.

The Snowtown Bodies in Barrels

May 1999

The bodies of eight murder victims were discovered in barrels filled with hydrochloric acid, in a small town in Australia called Snowtown. The barrels had been found inside a disused bank vault, and on discovery the room was filled with a horrific stench.

Some of the bodies had been cut into pieces, but none had been completely dissolved in the acid. Instead, they had become mummified, making identification easier. On further investigation, officers would find there were even more victims, reaching a total of twelve.

These horrific murders weren't just committed by one person – there were at least four people involved, possibly even more. The ringleader was a man named John Bunting, who had once been a neo-Nazi who held a deep abhorrence towards homosexuals and pedophiles. He was able to convince his

67

acquaintances to not only help kill the victims but also to assist with disposing of the bodies.

John Bunting was subsequently found guilty of committing 11 murders. Robert Wagner was convicted of committing 10 murders. A man who was mentally challenged, Mark Ray Haydon, was convicted of helping to dispose of the bodies and sentenced to 25 years in prison. Finally, a teenager who looked up to John Bunting and would do anything to impress him was found guilty of 4 of the murders.

All in the Family

March 2012

In Tuddern, Germany, neighbors called the police to report a terrible and peculiar smell emanating from a house occupied by a family of five. On investigation, local police discovered a horrifying crime scene with large vats filled with acid and a sludge material. On closer inspection, this sludge was found to contain fragments of bone.

The conclusion was reached that the perpetrators may have flushed some of this sludge down the toilet, and the sewage system of the small town was inspected. They found an alarming amount of body material that included bones from the feet and fingers, some located in the sewers a mile away from the home. Within the home they found gas masks, obviously used by the occupants of the house to protect themselves from the hydrochloric acid.

Police were able to determine that the family had killed two men, placed them in the vats, and filled them with the acid. The victims had been shot and hacked with an icepick to kill them. Three family members were apprehended, but two escaped and were believed to be on the run in South America.

The Killing of Karen Buckley

April 2015

Unlike most of the other acid cases, the murder of Buckley was completely random and a case of being in the wrong place at the wrong time. In the early hours of the morning, Karen crossed paths with a man named Alexander Pacteau outside a nightclub in Dumbarton Street, Glasgow, and within a matter of only 20 minutes, she would be dead.

Pacteau had managed to convince Karen to get into his car, and he drove her to nearby Kelvin Way where he proceeded to bash her over the head with a wrench and then strangle her. He took her back to the apartment he shared with a roommate and the roommate's mother and put a plan into place to cover what he had done.

One of the first things he did was dispose of the wrench in a nearby canal. He then purchased a large plastic barrel. He wrapped Karen's body in tape and bindings and placed her inside the barrel. He then poured a large amount of caustic soda, a type of acid, into the barrel. The barrel was then moved to a storage place.

What lead to the undoing of Pacteau was largely the efforts of the community and witnesses who had seen him talking to Karen outside the nightclub. He had also been recorded by CCTV purchasing large quantities of caustic soda, and it didn't take long for the police to catch up with him.

Although Pacteau admitted killing Karen, he has never explained why.

The End of a Wife

May 2015

Tricia Todd, a hospice nurse and US Air Force veteran, had been missing from Florida since April 27, 2015. She was meant to pick up her young daughter from a babysitter but never arrived. Her former husband, Steven Williams, a US airman who had been stationed in North Carolina, initially stated to police that he had been watching the child, but when Tricia didn't turn up he left the child with the babysitter and returned to his base

However, CCTV footage showed Williams driving Tricia's truck after she had gone missing, and as his story started to unravel, he became the number one suspect. When he finally admitted his involvement in her disappearance, he claimed they had argued about money and it had gotten physical. According to Williams, during the fight she had struck her head and died after he pushed her.

With Williams leading the way, the police were able to locate the shallow grave containing Tricia in the Hungryland Wildlife Management Area. It was a small hole, only around 3 feet in depth, with a container holding her remains. She had been cut up into pieces with a chainsaw, placed in the container, and submerged in acid.

By assisting police in finding her remains, Williams was able to negotiate a deal and plead no contest to a charge of second-degree murder. He was sentenced to 35 years in prison.

Copycat Killing in France

August 2015

In an apartment in Toulouse, the body of a French art student, Eva Bourseau, was found decomposing in acid. She had been placed into a plastic trunk-like container and covered in the acid, and her remains had been discovered by her mother, who was concerned after having no contact for two weeks.

It was discovered Eva had been murdered by three fellow students, after failing to pay her drug debt of more than £4.250. The three students had come up with the idea of placing her body in acid after seeing a similar scenario played out on a well-known television program, Breaking Bad.

71

Her body had been in the acid for around ten days before discovery, and during that period the murderers had returned to the apartment on numerous occasions to check on the rate of decomposition. To overcome the atrocious smell, they had used air fresheners so they could enter the apartment without being overcome by the stench.

Murder of an Officer

April 2016

This is perhaps one of the most gruesome of these murders involving acid. Officer Gordon Semple was a homosexual police officer in South London who frequented the gay dating scene, including online websites, despite having a live-in partner, Gary Meeks.

On April 1, Gordon disappeared while on duty, and his partner reported him missing that same night. It wasn't long before his mysterious disappearance would be explained, thanks to a neighbor being curious about an awful smell.

Stephen Harris lived in a block of apartments known as Peabody Estate, and when he noticed a terrible smell coming from a neighbor's residence, he called his brother to come and investigate for him. His brother Martin arrived and noticed the smell immediately. He approached the neighbor, an Italian by the name of Stefano Brizzi, and asked him what the smell was, to which he replied he was cooking for a friend. Naturally suspicious, Martin informed him they had called the police and they were on their way.

On arrival at the scene, police were horrified by what they discovered. In a bath of acid, parts of Gordon Semple were found dissolving. Other pieces of Gordon were boiling away on the stove, and Brizzi admitted he had also dumped parts of the body in the nearby Thames River. Despite their being no indications of cannibalism, the police couldn't help but notice the similarities to a serial killer Dennis Nilsen, who also murdered homosexual men and boiled them on the stove.

Apparently, Gordon had met Brizzi through a dating website and they had agreed to meet up. Brizzi claimed they had gotten into an argument and he had killed Gordon. Realizing he now had to dispose of the body, he decided to try a method shown on the television show, Breaking Bad, and purchased a large amount of acid.

It was taking too long for Gordon's remains to dissolve in the acid, so he decided to try other methods of disposal. Which is why parts were on the stove and parts were thrown in the river. Obviously Brizzi was charged with the murder of Gordon.

Summary of These Cases

It just goes to show, what you see on television isn't necessarily real. In more than one case, the idea of using acid came from a television show, and the murderers discovered it takes much longer to dissolve a human body in the acid than they thought. You can't blame the television show though— after all, if they had only looked at a little history they would have gotten the idea from John Haigh anyway.

It's also worth noting that no matter how many scented candles you light or how many cans of air freshener you spray around, you cannot disguise or hide the smell of a decomposing body. Because of the method of breaking down the fats and proteins with acid, the stench is multiplied ten-fold.

John Haigh may have been the first recorded serial killer to use acid as a means to dispose of his victims, but as these recent cases show, the idea is still very much out there.

CHAPTER 12:
John Haigh the Man and His Actions

No matter how hard we try, we cannot completely explain what made John tick, because he's not here to ask, and in-depth interviews weren't conducted back then like they are now. But we can certainly come up with some theories. What was it that helped shape him into the coldhearted killer he became? Was it really just about the money? Or was there more to John than we thought?

Nature, Nurture, or Both

As mentioned in previous chapters, there has been quite a bit of speculation over whether or not John was a victim of his environment or if he was just born a psychopath. Again, he can't be asked, and his parents most likely wouldn't have consented to interviews and discussions about their son, given their stern religious beliefs.

But by looking at other cases where the background is similar, it is possible to draw to some conclusions regarding his childhood and adult life. One has to be careful though, as it can be too easy to lump similarities into the same basket and call them fact. After all, it used to be believed that all serial killers came from broken homes where the family unit was divided, but we now know that is not always the case. John didn't come from a broken family, so he doesn't fit that basket.

Then consideration was given to the family and whether or not it was dysfunctional. There in itself is an issue, because who determines the level of dysfunction? Perhaps parents who were criminals, drug addicts, abusive and violent? But not every child that is abused or exposed to such criminal and addictive behavior becomes a killer. In many cases, the opposite occurs.

Could John's parents be considered dysfunctional? In some respects, yes. They were deeply religious and imposed a lot of restrictions on John. He became terrified of being a sinner, and his father wrought all sorts of fears on John's mind. Is this dysfunctional or trying to steer his son on the right paths in life? It's a debatable concept.

John's mother was considered to be the milder parent, with the roost being ruled by his father with a strong mind and stern voice. When John did misbehave, it was his mother who typically administered the punishment. Did he hate his mother? Apparently not. He also didn't despise his father. John didn't agree with their religious beliefs, but that was all.

If a child is isolated from friends and outside influences from a young age, this doesn't necessarily mean they will be unable to develop normal human relationships. John became an extremely charming and likeable young man who could strike a conversation with ease. He was so charming, in fact, that he was able to swindle a lot of people by convincing them to trust him.

Once John reached his late teens, he was able to work out for himself what he believed in regarding religion, and he was able to make decisions for himself. He embarked on journeys of sin, as his father would see it, and lived a normal life of a young adult. Apart from his notorious attempts at fraud and forgery, he seemed to be completely normal.

If his psychopathy wasn't borne from nurture, then one naturally looks at the theory of nature. Was John just born to be bad? Once again you must delve into his childhood to determine this. Typically with a natural born killer (as they are sometimes described) the signs show up during childhood, or at least adolescence. There are nine accepted signs of the potential to become a serial killer, so let's look at how John fits the list.

Antisocial behavior – John may have been isolated, but he certainly wasn't antisocial.

Arson – There are no indications that John ever set fire to anything.

Torturing small animals – John loved animals and cared more for them than people.

Poor family life – The family unit appeared to be strong, although perhaps a little strange.

Childhood abuse – There is no evidence that John was abused in any way as a child.

Substance abuse – John had the occasional alcoholic beverage but there was no alcohol or drug abuse.

Voyeurism – Rather than being interested in pornography, fetishism, or sadomasochism, John seemed to be not that interested in sex at all.

Intelligence – John was certainly intelligent but not necessarily at a higher level.

Shiftlessness – Perhaps this may fit John, as he flitted from job to job, but that was more likely due to his craving for more money rather than not being able to settle.

So when you look at the theories surrounding John, it is hard to determine whether John was deeply affected by nature or nurture. He showed absolutely no signs of being a troubled individual until he was actually caught after the murders. His family life was okay, albeit a little strict and odd. But in those religious circles his family environment was probably completely normal.

If a killer isn't affected by nature or nurture, then what is left? This is the most troubling question facing researchers today. People constantly want things to be black and white—born to kill or turned into a killer by environment. But sometimes things aren't that clear cut, and they fall into the grey area. John was most likely one of those. We will never know for sure, but it seems more likely that John was affected by both nature and nurture. Not because either was particularly bad, but because when combined, they may have altered his mindset about life, money and death.

The Money Motive

Although it seems like there haven't been a lot of killers who were motivated by money, it is estimated that anywhere from a quarter to a half of all murders are motivated by financial gain. However, it is not as common in serial killers, rather occurring in singular murders.

The definition of money as a motive for murder is clarified as a serial killer who commits multiple murders as a means to gain access to their money. This includes those who kill during the act of robbery, provided they continue to kill for the same reason. A serial killer that kills for money will often choose victims that are known to him, as it is easier to gain access to their financial records, papers, and accounts.

In some cases the killer will take out insurance policies on the selected victim before the murder is committed. This is a more common method for murders with money as a motive, and is typically seen in situations involving family members or close friends. It is harder to use this method with victims that are unknown or not as close, as the insurance payout could open up a lot of questions. In cases where a spouse goes missing or is killed, the first thing the investigators look at is whether or not there is an insurance policy and when that policy was activated.

With John, the motive appears to be purely financial gain. He killed because he was greedy, not because he felt an overwhelming urge to kill. Even though he tried to convince the jury that he got urges to kill, driven by disturbing dreams and a lust for blood, it was clear that this wasn't the case. John only killed when he started running out of funds. As soon as the money dried up, he would start looking for his next victim. He also only killed those he knew had a significant level of wealth.

If he had been driven to kill by the thrill, he wouldn't have had the ability to take his time selecting a victim, and he certainly wouldn't have been so choosy about their financial status. It is true that with some serial killers the initial motive may be money, but after time they become more addicted to the thrill of the kill. This is where the victims start to become more random and more frequent. This definitely wasn't the case for John. He never wavered from his plan and choice of victim.

To kill for money takes a particularly cold person, as there is no emotional force behind the murder, simply the need to have more. Unlike killers who are driven by emotions such as love, revenge, sex, and anger, money motive killers are often harder to detect and apprehend. There is nothing linking the suspect to the victim to suggest murderous intent, apart from a friendship or being acquainted.

John specifically chose his victims, took his time planning the kills, and put a lot of thought into how he was going to use their identification to gain access over their money and property. He didn't just wake up one morning and decide to go out and kill a person because he felt like it. He waited until in his mind the kill was necessary to financially support his lifestyle. This makes John a much colder and more devious killer.

Victim Selection

Each of John's six known victims were his acquaintances. Some he had known for a period of time, such as the McSwann family. Of the six, the murders of William McSwann and his elderly parents were the most disturbing, given they had a history between them.

John had worked for William for a year as his driver and laborer at his fairground. When John had left his employment, William told him he would always be welcome back if he wanted to return to the job. Later, when they met up again by chance, they spent a lot of time socializing with each other, even going to the local pub together for a beer on numerous occasions.

William thought so highly of John that he didn't hesitate to take him home to meet his parents. After all, John was his friend. His parents liked John just as much and opened their home to him for visits, and they were happy to share sensitive information about their wealth with him. Nobody ever expected John to have such a terrible motive for maintaining the friendship.

Despite the strong and long friendship with William, John didn't hesitate to kill him and put him in the barrel of acid. The majority of people couldn't comprehend doing such a thing, especially when there had been no arguments, disputes, or bad dealings between the two men. There was no emotional 'bad blood' between them at all—William was simply a means to an end for John, and that end was money.

Then, to make things even worse, John concocted a far-fetched but relatively plausible story to explain William's disappearance to his parents. To continue his ruse, John would write postcards and letters from William (who was supposedly in hiding) to his parents to reassure them that he was alive and well. Until John wanted more money.

By killing William's parents, John not only gained access to their money and properties, but it also enabled him to fully access William's as well. He was now able to collect William's checks, and when combined with what he had gained from the elderly McSwanns, he was finally able to live the high life he so desired.

While living frivolously on his ill-gotten gains, John became aware that the money wouldn't last forever, so he had to find another victim. He was in no rush, as he still had regular income from William's death coming in, but he needed to plan ahead. As fate would have it, he found the next victim when answering an ad for a property that was up for sale.

This is how he met the Hendersons. Although he was unable to purchase their property due to lack of funds, he was able to add them to his list of potential victims after seeing displays of wealth throughout their home. It would be a while before they met again, but by then John was ready.

The Hendersons thought John was a friendly guy, and it didn't take much at all for them to share with him the details regarding their considerable wealth. This sealed their fate as far as John was concerned. After he murdered Dr. Henderson, he went straight back for Mrs. Henderson. Now, for some killers, getting rid of the husband would be enough, as they could then move in and swindle the grieving widow. But, John didn't want to risk leaving behind a potential witness, so she had to go too.

The murder of Olive Durand-Deacon would lead to John's undoing. He had befriended her, often having tea with her in a public setting, and this is what led to him becoming a suspect. Olive was very wealthy and was a bit of a 'show off', always wearing a variety of sparkling jewels along with furs and an expensive Persian lambskin coat. She was a single woman, somewhat lonely, and this is why she became what John thought was a perfect victim.

Unfortunately for John, too many people knew about his friendship with Olive, and due to his inability to keep telling a straight lie, it wasn't long before he was caught. When the full story came out as to how many people John had killed for money, everyone was shocked. He had appeared to be a nice gentleman, well-dressed, superbly mannered, and utterly charming. But this was all part of his plan. To get close to those he wanted to, he had to appear to be of the same social standing as them. He was quite the actor and managed to pull his plan off for too long. However, the six known victims weren't the only ones in his line of sight.

There was a woman he had attended school with that John made contact with much later in life. By reading the obituaries in the paper, he had learned she had suffered a recent death in the family and that she was a widow. John sent her a letter saying that he would like to come and visit her. She was quite pleased with the letter and thought it was a very sweet thing for him to do given they hadn't seen each other in many years. Unfortunately for John, she died before he was able to visit. It would be easy to assume that this poor woman had been an intended victim, and that for John nature had beaten him to it.

There was also the possibility that his girlfriend, Barbara Stephens, had been on John's potential victims list. He had been seeing her for quite some time and had proposed the idea of marriage to her. Barbara always felt something wasn't quite right though, and when John was arrested for the murders, she couldn't help but wonder if she was going to be next. When she questioned John in prison he certainly didn't deny it.

Every single victim of John's was someone he knew—a person he had formed some type of relationship with. He took his time and gleaned as much information from each victim as he deemed necessary to take full control of their finances after their death. He planned, plotted, and schemed, choosing each victim carefully to maximize his own wealth, all because he wanted to live the high life and pay off his gambling debts.

CHAPTER 13:
In the Media

Many serial killers are written about in books, portrayed in movies, and sung about in pop music, and John was no different.

In Audio Stories

'The Jar of Acid', 1951 — part of a radio series called The Black Museum

'In Conversation with an Acid Bath Murderer', 2011 — an audio drama

In Television and Movies

'A is For Acid' — a television drama

'Psychoville' — John Haigh appears as a vision to psychopath David Sowerbutts.

'Criminal Minds' — although not referenced by name, the fictitious character Henry Grace was very similar to John.

Video Games

'Clock Tower' — a fictional version of John is a boss character in this video game.

Music

'Acid Bath Vampire' — a song by Macabre, an American thrash/death metal band.

'Make Them Die Slowly (John George Haigh)'— a song by Church of Misery, a Japanese doom metal band.

Art

'Madame Tussaud's' – a waxwork figure of John was created and displayed in the 'Chamber of Horrors' display at Madame Tussaud's.

Conclusion

There are those out there who don't find people like John who kill for money as interesting as those that kill for other reasons. Perhaps it's because those who kill out of revenge always have more of a story behind their actions, or those that kill random people for the thrill of it are more interesting, as they seem to be completely irrational and unexplainable.

There is no real question as to why John killed William McSwann, his parents, the Hendersons, and Olive Durand-Deacon. He was greedy and had a sense of entitlement that was beyond comprehension. He believed he was meant to have fancy cars, flashy clothes, and a lifestyle to be envied by others. He just didn't want to earn it the legitimate way.

While it's true John's childhood may have had some influence on his behavior later in life, it doesn't explain how or why he became the icy-hearted killer that he was. There was no deep psychological problem or mental illness to explain his character. He wasn't trying to right some deep-seated wrong or seek revenge against a foe. He was just downright guilty.

The story of John Haigh is far more interesting than many would think at close glance. It wasn't just that he killed to line his own pockets. John killed people he knew, those who thought he was a friend or a pleasant acquaintance. He used every deceptive tactic he could muster to sway them to follow him to his workshop, and they all went willingly.

From the time he was arrested until the day he was executed, John continued to try and convince anyone who would listen that he was insane. The nightmares, the blood, the drinking of his own urine—these were all part of his dastardly plan. But an insane individual could not have carried out acts such as those committed by him and get away with it for so long. An insane individual wouldn't have had the ability to put so much thought into the planning. With his own intelligence, John had inadvertently proven he was sane.

John's plan to murder for money had almost been foolproof. His only mistake was killing a woman who would be missed right away—before he had time to come up with more lies and deception. Olive Durand-Deacon would be his last victim and the one who saw him executed.

More books by Jack Rosewood

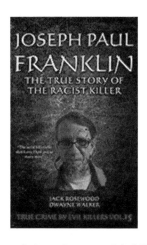

Among the annals of American serial killers, few were as complex and prolific as Joseph Paul Franklin. At a gangly 5'11, Franklin hardly looked imposing, but once he put a rifle in his hands and an interracial couple in his cross hairs, Joseph Paul Franklin was as deadly as any serial killer. In this true crime story you will learn about how one man turned his hatred into a vocation of murder, which eventually left over twenty people dead across America. Truly, Franklin's story is not only that of a true crime serial killer, but also one of racism in America as he chose Jews, blacks, and especially interracial couples as his victims.

Joseph Paul Franklin's story is unique among serial killers biographies because he gained no sexual satisfaction from his murders and there is no indication that he was ever compelled to kill. But make no mistake about it, by all definitions; Joseph Paul Franklin was a serial killer. In fact, the FBI stated that Franklin was the first known racially motivated serial killer in the United States: he planned to kill as many of his perceived enemies as possible in order to start an epic race war across the country. An examination of Franklin's life will reveal how he became a racially motivated serial killer and the steps he took to carry out his one man war against the world.

Open the pages of this e-book to read a disturbing story of true crime murder in America's heartland. You will be disturbed and perplexed at Franklin's murderous campaign as he made himself a one man death squad, eliminating as many of his political enemies that he could. But you will also be captivated with Franklin's shrewdness and cunning as he avoided the authorities for years while he carried out his diabolical plot!

The world can be a very strange place in general and when you open the pages of this true crime anthology you will quickly learn that the criminal world specifically can be as bizarre as it is dangerous. In the following book, you will be captivated by mysterious missing person cases that defy all logic and a couple cases of murderous mistaken identity. Follow along as detectives conduct criminal investigations in order to solve cases that were once believed to be unsolvable. Every one of the crime cases chronicled in the pages of this book are as strange and disturbing as the next.

The twelve true crime stories in this book will keep you riveted as you turn the pages, but they will probably also leave you with more questions than answers. For instance, you will be left pondering how two brothers from the same family could disappear with no trace in similar circumstances over ten years apart. You will also wonder how two women with the same first and last names, but with no personal connections, could be murdered within the same week in the same city. The examination of a number of true crime murder cases that went cold, but were later solved through scientific advances, will also keep you intrigued and reading.

Open the pages of this book, if you dare, to read some of the most bizarre cases of disappearances, mistaken identity, and true murder. Some of the cases will disturb and anger you, but make no mistake, you will want to keep reading!

According to statistics, at least 50 to 100 serial killers are currently roaming the United States, traveling highways and backroads in search of their next victims.

This true crime box set unites the stories of some of the most sadistic killers in United States history into one fascinating collection that vividly reveals their bloody reigns of terror.

California resident William Bonin, who had a genius IQ and could have done anything with his life, instead enlisted his friends to help him lure young men into the back of his blue Ford Econoline van, where he tortured his victims so sadistically that one died of shock from the pain and sheer brutality of his attack.

In Texas, praline candy maker Dean Corll also had a proclivity for young men, and plied his teenage accomplices with drugs and booze so that they would bring their friends to his house for a party, although Corll was the only one having any fun.

After using drugs and alcohol to subdue his victims - sometimes boys from families who'd already lost one son to the madman - he would cuff them to a wooden board so they could be raped and tortured in ways that would give anyone nightmares.

Brothers James Jr. and Linwood Briley were also a gruesome team. After watching them torture the exotic animals they collected, James Briley Sr. was so terrified of his two oldest sons that he locked his doors at night for fear that he might become their next victim. The elder Briley was right to be afraid, because at 16, Linwood shot his elderly neighbor from his bedroom window as she hung her laundry outside, then casually said, "I heard she had heart problems, she would have died soon anyway."

While many serial killers are unable to work alone, others see their work as a solitary art.

This collection of true crime stories brings together the worst of both types, those who enlist the help of others to perform their dastardly deeds, and those who kill alone.

Donald "Pee Wee" Gaskins committed his first murder in prison in a desperate bid to appear tough enough to prevent the rapes and torture that were commonplace for him, but by the time he got out of prison, he was done being a victim, and he cruised the Atlantic coast in search of both male and female victims, killing so many that he earned the nickname "the Meanest Man in the World."

Robert Berdella, the owner of Bob's Bizarre Bazaar in Kansas City, also worked alone, and enjoying luring friends and male prostitutes home, only to hold them captive in his basement, torturing them until they died, then disposing of their dismembered remains at a local landfill, where they have never been found. It wasn't until a seventh kidnap victim escaped through a basement window wearing only a dog collar, sneaking out while Berdella ran his store of oddities, that police caught the man who kept a detail log and photographs of his horrifying crimes.

These six serial killer biographies travel decades and miles, bringing your worst nightmares to life. A true crime anthology that's truly the stuff of nightmares, this boxed set is one that you'll want to read during those moments when you forget that the monsters are real, and could be living right next door.

This True Crime Box Set includes the following books

- Robert Berdella: The True Story of The Kansas City Butcher
- Dean Corll: The True Story of The Houston Mass Murders
- Donald Gaskins: The Meanest Man In America

- The Briley Brothers: The True Story of The Slaying Brothers
- Martin Bryant: The Port Arthur Massacre
- William Bonin: The True Story of The Freeway Killer

GET THESE BOOKS FOR FREE

Go to <u>www.jackrosewood.com</u>
and get these E-Books for free!

A Note From The Author

Hello, this is Jack Rosewood. Thank you for reading this true crime story. I hope you enjoyed the read of this chilling story. If you did, I'd appreciate if you would take a few moments to post a review on Amazon.

I would also love if you'd sign up to my newsletter to receive updates on new releases, promotions and a FREE copy of my Herbert Mullin E-Book, go to www.JackRosewood.com

Thanks again for reading this book, make sure to follow me on Facebook.

Best Regards

Jack Rosewood

Printed in Great Britain
by Amazon